Easy
Arabic Script
a step-by-step guide to handwriting

Jane Wightwick and Mahmoud Gaafar

Illustrations by Mahmoud Gaafar

Contributions and handwriting models
by Professor Mohammed Hamaam
Head of the Academy of Arabic Script, Cairo

D1414760

McGraw·Hill

New York   Chicago   San Francisco   Lisbon   London   Madrid   Mexico City
Milan   New Delhi   San Juan   Seoul   Singapore   Sydney   Toronto

The **McGraw·Hill** Companies

Also in this series
Easy Arabic Grammar, *Jane Wightwick and Mahmoud Gaafar*

First published in North America 2005 by McGraw-Hill

First published in Great Britain 2005 by Palgrave Macmillan, Houndmills, Basingstoke, Hampshire RG21 6XS

ISBN: 978-0-071-46209-9

This book is printed on paper suitable for recycling and made from fully managed and sustained forest sources.

Library of Congress Catalog Card Number: On file

Printed and bound in China

Contents

Acknowledgements

The authors and publishers wish to thank the following
for use of copyright material: Dar Assayad for the use of
the masthead from *Al Anwar* newspaper; Professor
Mohammed Hamaam for the sample of his calligraphy.

Every effort has been made to trace all copyright holders,
but if any have been inadvertently overlooked, the
publishers will be pleased to make the necessary
arrangements at the first opportunity.

Introduction

The history of the Arabic script

The Arabic alphabet and written language has remained remarkably constant since the sixth or seventh century AD, largely due to the unifying factor of the Qur'an. There is no clear documented progression in the development of the script before this time and only a limited number of original pre-Islamic Arabic texts exist, sometimes as scraps of stone or parchment.

Arabic is a Semitic language related to Aramaic and Hebrew. The language has its roots in the nomadic oral tradition of the desert, which largely explains the lack of early examples of the script.

Although spoken Arabic dialects have diverged in the same way that Romance languages such as Italian and French have diverged from Latin, the Modern Standard Arabic of today's media is close to the language of the Qur'an and Classical literature. The spelling and grammar have not changed significantly over the centuries.

Different styles of writing

Arabic calligraphy is a highly respected art form with hundreds of different styles. Many of these calligraphic styles are very ornate and intended more for decoration than comprehension. The calligrapher relies on the reader already knowing the text, often a verse from the Qur'an, and can concentrate on making the script as beautiful and balanced as possible.

As far as everyday written Arabic is concerned, there are two significant styles: *naskh*, the basic script used for most printed material; and *ruq'a*, the script used for most handwritten material. Although it is possible to typeset *ruq'a* or handwrite

An example of highly decorative calligraphy showing text from the
Qur'an (Professor Mohammed Hamaam, Head of the Academy of
Arabic Script, Cairo)

naskh, this does not happen commonly.

Most Arab children will initially learn to read and write *naskh*
in a similar way to English children learning to read and write
using infant letters. At about 11 or 12 years old, secondary
school students in the Arab world will graduate to writing *ruq'a*,
which is an eagerly anticipated step and a sign of having
joined the 'adult' club.

Ruq'a is a more flowing script than *naskh* and designed for
speed and efficiency. Good handwriting is much admired as an

extension of the respect paid to calligraphy. As a learner you will find a mastery of the *ruq'a* script will help you to be regarded as a serious student of the language, as well as being a more efficient way of handwriting.

This book sets out to compare and contrast *naskh* and *ruq'a* and to teach you a fluid and mature *ruq'a* writing style, using models produced by one of the leading experts on handwriting in the Arab world and providing extensive practice material.

There are obvious similarities between *naskh* and *ruq'a*, but there are also some important differences to be mastered when writing *ruq'a*. For example, *ruq'a* script largely floats above the line whereas elements of *naskh* fall below the line. Also, many of the fiddlier and more time-consuming elements of *naskh* are rationalised in *ruq'a* for the sake of speed. For example the separate dots above and below the main script are joined together.

الياء في أول الكلمة وفي وسطها هي:

الباء والتاء والثاء والنون

السِاءِ في أول الكلمة وفي وسطها هي:

الباءِ والتَاءِ والثَاءِ والنون

A sentence written in both scripts. The *naskh* version (top) was typeset and the *ruq'a* version (below) was handwritten by Professor Hamaam. Can you spot the similarities and differences?

How to use this book

This script book can be beneficial at different stages of the learning process. It can be used by complete beginners who wish to master the *ruq'a* script simultaneously with the printed *naskh*, supplementing the early stages of study of the Arabic language, whether in a classroom or home setting. Beginners often find the script quite easy to master in principle but still find it takes a long time to become fluent in reading and writing. This book can help you overcome the script barrier much more quickly.

Alternatively, you may have already studied Arabic and be proficient in reading *naskh*. But you may not yet have had the opportunity to improve your own writing or to decipher the handwriting of native speakers. This book can take you to the next level by concentrating on making your Arabic handwriting more mature and fluent.

At whatever stage you approach this book, it is best to work your way through the units methodically. There are three main parts to the book. The first part covers how to form and join individual letter shapes; the second covers special combinations of letters; and the third part is an activity section for further practice. Features included are:

- clear explanation and graphics showing how the letter shapes are formed

- numerous practice exercises to help you achieve fluency in writing

- *Master calligrapher tips*: expert hints on writing in *ruq'a* from Professor Mohammed Hamaam, head of the Academy of Arabic Script in Cairo. Follow the instructions in this guide and you will have good *ruq'a* handwriting. Follow Professor Hamaam's tips and you will have even better *ruq'a* writing!

- *'extra'* sections covering features of the Arabic script such as writing vowels and hamza (ء)

- photos and illustrations showing the script in context

- *Write on!*: additional stimulating and useful activities to improve recognition and fluency of writing.

Basic principles of Arabic script

There are a few basic principles of Arabic script which apply whichever style of writing is used:

- There are 28 letters in the alphabet.
- The script is written right to left.
- There are no capital letters.
- Words are written in cursive, or 'joined up', writing. All letters join to the letter before in a word and all but six join to the letter after also.

Once you have mastered the various forms of each letter shape in both *naskh* and *ruq'a* you will find you can write and read Arabic in most everyday contexts.

Finally, make sure you have a good ink pen, drawing pen, gel pen or a soft pencil to write Arabic. The Arabic script usually looks better when written with a thicker nib or tip. Arabic is a flowing script and it is difficult to achieve a good hand with a cheap biro.

part

1

Basic letter shapes

For the first few units of Part 1, you will be practising how to write individual Arabic shapes and letters. When you have mastered enough letters, we will introduce complete words to recognise and copy.

Practise forming the letter shape above, first by tracing the shape and then by copying what you see. Pay special attention to where you start the shape.

This shape is used for three different Arabic letters. Compare the printed and the handwritten versions:

Printed form   Handwritten form

the letter bā'. The basic shape with one dot underneath. Pronounced 'b' as in 'boat'.

the letter tā'. The basic shape with two dots above. Pronounced 't' as in 'tin'.

the letter thā'. The basic shape
with three dots above.
Pronounced 'th' as in 'thanks'.

Notice that in the handwritten form the dots become joined up
for speed.

Two dots are joined like this: ➖

Three dots are joined like this: ∧

Practise tracing and copying those shapes by themselves,
remembering to move your pen from right to left.

∧ ➖ ∧ ➖ ∧ ➖ ∧ ➖ ∧ ➖ ∧ ➖

Now practise all three letters. Always complete the main letter
shape first and then add any 'dots'.

ب ب ←

ت ت ←

ث ث ←

Joining up

Arabic is a cursive script: most Arabic letters are written joined up to the other letters in a word. Here is how the letter shape for ب, ت and ث looks when at the beginning, in the middle, and at the end of a word:

final	**medial**	**initial**
joined to the	*joined both sides*	*joined to the*
letter before only		*letter after only*

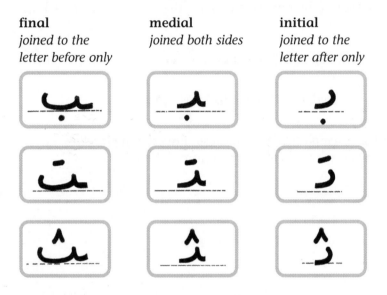

Notice how in the initial and medial positions, the dots associated with the letter move to the right of the shape, sitting above or under the right-hand curve.

 Master calligrapher tips

The shape of the initial bā', tā' and thā' is one of the most important in Arabic writing. The stroke is fundamental to handwriting and forms the basis of a number of Arabic letter shapes. Pay attention to the starting and finishing positions.

This letter shape can be joined together in different combinations. Compare the printed and handwritten combinations below:

Printed form   Handwritten form

بث   ‫ـبِثـ‬   = ث + ب   ←(read right to left)

تب   ‫ـتَبـ‬   = ب + ت

تبث   ‫ـتَبِثـ‬   = ث + ب + ت

Practise copying the shapes without dots and then the combinations of letters. Complete the *whole* combination from *right to left* before adding any 'dots', also from *right to left*.

ـب   ـد   د   ـب   ـد   د

← بث تَب تَبِث بِث تَب تَبِث

This letter shape is used for only one Arabic letter:

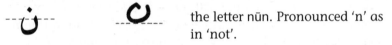

Printed form   *Handwritten form*

ن   ن   the letter nūn. Pronounced 'n' as in 'not'.

The printed naskh form of nūn falls below the line, but the handwritten ruq'a form tends to sit more *on* the line. The dot above is often joined to the main letter shape in handwriting.

Practise tracing and then copying the shape.

start
here

Joining up

nūn has exactly the same shape as bā' when in the initial or medial position (see Unit 1), except it has one dot *above*. Beginners can confuse nūn and bā'. Remember b̲ā' has the dot b̲elow.

final	**medial**	**initial**
joined to the letter before only	*joined both sides*	*joined to the letter after only*

Printed form   Handwritten form

ثبن   نِـبِث   = ث + ب + ن

تنب   بِنِتَ   = ت + ن + ب

نب   عر   = ن + ب

Notice that when joining to a final nūn, as in the final example above, you need to start the previous letter higher to end up back on the line. Practise copying the combinations below:

Master calligrapher tips

You can also write the isolated and final nūn like this:

So the combination ب followed by ن could also be written:

بن من اليمن bunn min al-yaman (Coffee beans from Yemen)

ي

This letter shape represents the Arabic letter yā':

Printed form   *Handwritten form*

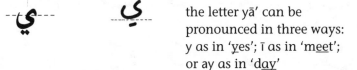

the letter yā' can be
pronounced in three ways:
y as in 'yes'; ī as in 'meet';
or ay as in 'day'

Like the nūn, the printed naskh form of yā' falls below the line,
but the handwritten ruq'a form sits *on* the line. The two dots
below become joined in handwriting as with ت (see Unit 1)

Practise tracing and then copying the shape.

start
here

Joining up

yā' is another letter which has exactly the same shape as ب (see
Unit 1) when in the initial or medial position, except that it has
two dots *below*. In the final position, it looks similar to the
isolated letter.

final	**medial**	**initial**
joined to the letter before only	*joined both sides*	*joined to the letter after only*

To summarise, there are *five* letters which share the same shape in their initial and medial positions, and are only distinguished by the number of dots above or below:

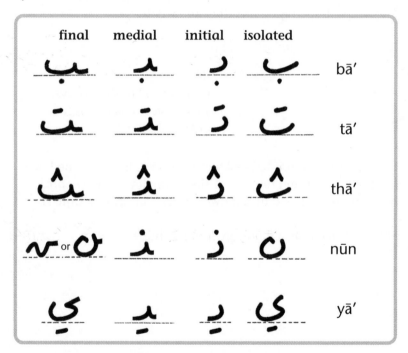

final	medial	initial	isolated	
ـب	ـبـ	بـ	ب	bā'
ـت	ـتـ	تـ	ت	tā'
ـث	ـثـ	ثـ	ث	thā'
ـن or	ـنـ	نـ	ن	nūn
ـي	ـيـ	يـ	ي	yā'

Notice how these combinations are written:

Printed form   Handwritten form

بيت   ـبيتَ   = ت + ي + ب ←

ثيب   ـثِيب   = ب + ي + ث

ين   or يـن   = ن + ي

نـي   ـنـي   = ن + ي

Sometimes a final yā' is written without the dots and
pronounced 'a', as in the names منى mona or ليلى layla. In
addition, some people don't bother to handwrite the dots on
the final yā' even when they should be there!

Practise tracing and copying the combinations below.

← بيت بيت بيت بيت بيت

← ثيب ثيب ثيب ثيب ثيب

جـ جـ جـ جـ جـ جـ جـ جـ ←

جـ جـ جـ جـ جـ جـ جـ جـ ←

لي لي لي لي لي لي لي لي ←

لي لي لي لي لي لي لي لي ←

بيت التين bayt at-tīn (House of Figs)

تين من العلمين tīn min al-ɛalamayn (Figs from El Alamein)

Notice that the 'dots' over or under the script may move
around in handwriting, sometimes ending up to the left of
where they should be (see the dots on التين above). This
movement happens because the dots are added *after* the main
word has been completed and is comparable to what happens
in English handwriting when you might find the cross stroke of
a 't' has moved to the right.

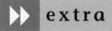

Vowel and doubling signs

Most modern Arabic is written without short vowels, in a similar way to the language of mobile text messages ('cn u cm tdy?'). So a word such as بنت bint (girl) is actually written as bnt and بيت bayt (house) as byt.

It is possible to add signs above and below the main script showing the short vowels, and these are sometimes included for clarity or in material aimed at learners, as well as being a feature of classical and religious texts.

The vowel signs are:

فتحة faṭha   a dash above, pronounced as a short 'a' *after* the letter, for example ...ـبَ ba

ضمّة ḍamma   a comma-shape above, pronounced as a short 'u' after the letter, for example ...ـبُ bu

كسرة kasra   a dash below, pronounced as a short 'i' after the letter, for example ...ـبِ bi

There are also two additional signs:

سكون sukūn   a small circle above showing that *no vowel* follows the letter, e.g. بِنْت bint (girl)

شدّة shadda   a small 'w' shape above showing that the letter is *doubled*, e.g. بُنّ bunn (coffee beans)

Don't confuse these signs with the dots above and below letters. The dots are an integral part of the script, distinguishing one letter from another. The vowels and doubling signs are a discretionary feature.

Practise writing the signs, following the direction of the arrow, and making sure you move your pen from right to left. Only kasra (i) is written under the line:

Now practise tracing and copying these words with the vowel and doubling signs included. Follow these steps:
1. Complete the main shape of the word.
2. Add the letter dots from right to left.
3. Add the vowel and doubling signs from right to left.

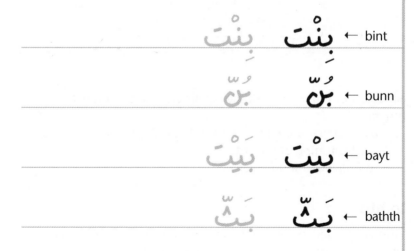

← bint

← bunn

← bayt

← bathth

The letter alif is the first letter of the Arabic alphabet and one of the simplest to recognise and write: a single downward stroke.

Printed form   *Handwritten form*

Practise tracing and then copying the shape.

start here

alif does not represent a single consistent sound. It has two functions:
- as a 'carrier' for one of the short vowels (a, u, i), usually at the beginning of a word
- to indicate a long ā vowel.

Joining up

Most Arabic letters join to the letters either side of them in a word. alif is one of six Arabic letters that *only join to the letter before* (on its right). This effectively means that the alif retains its shape wherever it falls in a word, with just a small joining stroke if it is joined to the letter before.

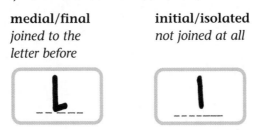

medial/final
*joined to the
letter before*

initial/isolated
not joined at all

The letter following an alif (to the left) must be written in the initial form, or in the isolated form if it is the only remaining letter in the word.

An alif at the beginning of a word is usually written with a hamza symbol (ء) over it if the vowel is a or u, or under it if the vowel is i:

a or u: أ   i: إ

Complete the whole word before adding the hamza (see *extra* section pages 42–3 for more details on hamza).

Look carefully at how these words are written:

Printed form   Handwritten form

بـاب   باب   bāb *door*

أب   أب   ab *father*

بابـا   بابا   bābā *daddy/papa*

إن   إن   in *if*

أنا   أنا   anā *I (am)*

نباتي   نباتي   nabātī *vegetarian*

Practise tracing and then copying those words containing alif.

باب   باب   باب   باب   باب   ←

أَب   أَب   أَب   أَب   أَب   ←

لَب   لَب   لَب   لَب   لَب   ←

إِن   إِن   إِن   إِن   إِن   ←

أَبًا   أَبًا   أَبًا   أَبًا   أَبًا   ←

← نباتي   نباتي   نباتي   نباتي   نباتي

بابا – أنا في بيت ثابت bābā – anā fī bayt thābit
(Daddy – I'm in Thabit's house)

 ر ز و

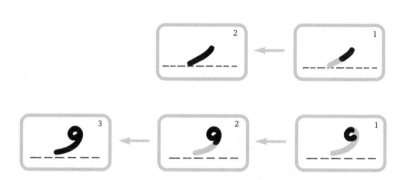

The two letter shapes above are very similar. The downwards sloping stroke used to produce ر has a small 'head' added to produce the و shape.

Printed form   Handwritten form

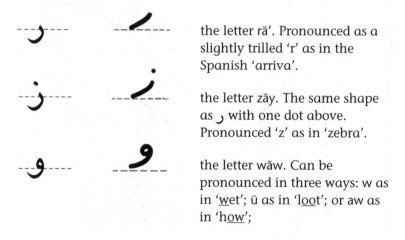

the letter rā'. Pronounced as a slightly trilled 'r' as in the Spanish 'arriva'.

the letter zāy. The same shape as ر with one dot above. Pronounced 'z' as in 'zebra'.

the letter wāw. Can be pronounced in three ways: w as in '<u>w</u>et'; ū as in 'l<u>oo</u>t'; or aw as in 'h<u>ow</u>';

Notice that although the printed naskh letters fall *under* the line the handwritten ruq'a letters finish *on* the line – one of the fundamental differences between the two scripts.

Practise tracing and then copying the letter shapes.

Joining up

rā', zāy and wāw are three more letters like alif that *only join to the letter before* (on the right) in a word.

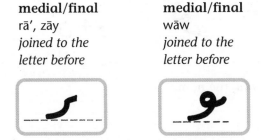

medial/final
rā', zāy
joined to the
letter before

medial/final
wāw
joined to the
letter before

Remember that after non-joining letters, the following letter in a word must be written in the initial or isolated form, depending on whether it is the final letter in the word. Look at how the Arabic names on the next page are written.

Printed form   Handwritten form

نور   نور   nūr

زين   زين   zayn

أنور   أنور   anwar

زينب   زينب   zaynab

✒ **Master calligrapher tips**

Because the shapes of the handwritten ر and و sit *on* the line
in ruq'a, you should try to raise the letter before so that you
end up back in the right position:

$$بر = ر + ب$$

$$نو = و + ن$$

Practise copying the names.

← نور نور نور زين زين

← أُنور   أُنور   أُنور   أُنور

← زينب زينب زينب زينب

Whose peg is whose? How many names can you read?

6 د ذ د

This letter shape looks similar to ر but is rounder. It is used for two Arabic letters.

Printed form   *Handwritten form*

the letter dāl. Pronounced 'd' as in 'den'.

the letter dhāl. The same shape with one dot above. Pronounced 'th' as in 'th' or 'that'.

✒ **Master calligrapher tips**

The stroke used to write the handwritten د is the same as that used for the initial ب or تـ, etc.:

Practise tracing and then copying dāl and dhāl.

start
here

Joining up

dāl and dhāl are the last of the six letters that *don't* join to the next letter in a word. Here is a summary of all six letters in their isolated form and when joined to the letter before:

final/medial	isolated	
ـل	ا	alif
ـد	ـد	dāl
ـذ	ـذ	dhāl
ـر	ـر	rā'
ـز	ـز	zay
ـو	ـو	wāw

Notice how these combinations are written:

Printed form   Handwritten form

Printed	Handwritten	
بد	ـبـد	← ب + د =
برد	بـرد	ب + ر + د =
ذي	ذي	ذ + ي =
ذباب	ذباب	ذ + ا + ب + ب =
يدين	يديـن	ي + د + ي + ن =

Note that even with non-joining letters, it is usually quicker to finish the whole word before adding any dots right to left:

Step 1: دباب

Step 2: ذباب

بريد عادي barīd ɛādī
(Ordinary mail)

Practise tracing and then copying the words.

← بد بد بد بد بد بد

← برد برد برد برد برد

← ذي ذي ذي ذي ذي

← ذباب ذباب ذباب ذباب

← يدين يدين يدين يدين يدين

▶▶ extra

Long vowels

You have met the short vowel marks on pages 14–15. These marks are written above and below the main script and are discretionary.

However, if a vowel is long, for example a long ū as in 'b<u>oo</u>t', this requires an additional letter to be added to the word:

long ā (as in 'f<u>a</u>ther')   ا alif added after the letter: بﺎ bā

long ū (as in 'b<u>oo</u>t')   و wāw added after the letter: بو bū

long ī (as in 'm<u>ee</u>t')   ي yā' added after the letter: بي bī

Look at the handwritten and printed versions of the words below which contain long vowels. Remember:

- ا alif and و wāw do not join to the *following* letter

- ي yā' has the same shape as ب in the intial and medial forms, except it has two dots under.

You will also occasionally see a long ā written as a wavy sign (مدّة madda) over an alif: آ, as in آنسة ānisa (young woman).

Printed form   Handwritten form

باب	ـبـاب	bāb *door/gate*
نور	نور	nūr *light (also a name)*
دين	دين	dīn *religion*
بريد	بريد	barīd *mail*
نار	نار	nār *fire*
ياباني	ياباني	yābānī *Japanese*

Practise writing the words containing long vowels.

باب

نور

دين

بريد

نار

ياباني

مبروك يا حبيبتي!

mabrūk yā ḥabībatī!

(Congratulations darling!)

Start this letter shape a little above the line, then loop round clockwise and add the curved tail. The movement is a little like a mirror-image figure of 8.

Practise tracing and then copying the letter shape.

start here ➞

This shape is used for three Arabic letters. Notice the difference between the printed and handwritten forms:

Printed form   Handwritten form

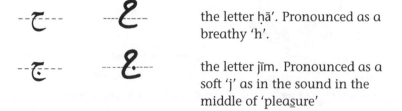

the letter ḥā'. Pronounced as a breathy 'h'.

the letter jīm. Pronounced as a soft 'j' as in the sound in the middle of 'pleasure'

--خ--   ---خ----   the letter khā'. Pronounced at the back of the throat. Similar to the 'ch' in the Scottish word 'lo<u>ch</u>'.

Joining up

Joining ḥā', jīm and khā' requires practice.

final	**medial**	**initial**
joined to the letter before only	*joined both sides*	*joined to the letter after only*

The intial form of the shape is relatively straightforward, but when other letters are handwritten before ḥā', jīm or khā' they tend to be placed *above,* so that they end up joining at the top left of the shape. Look at the examples below:

Printed form   Handwritten form

جا ‎ ‎ ‎ --جا-- ‎ ‎ ‎ = ا + ج

حو ‎ ‎ ‎ --حو-- ‎ ‎ ‎ = و + ح

بح ‎ ‎ ‎ --بح-- ‎ ‎ ‎ = ح + ب

ريح ‎ ‎ ‎ --ريح-- ‎ ‎ ‎ = ح + ي + ر

أخ ‎ ‎ ‎ --أخ-- ‎ ‎ ‎ = خ + أ

In this unit, we'll concentrate on the initial and isolated forms.

The isolated form is used when the letter *follows* one of the six non-joining letters (see Unit 6 for summary table) *and* is the last letter in a word, as in أخ on page 31.

Part 2 of this book deals with combination shapes and you can practise the medial and final combinations for ḥā', jīm and khā' in Unit 17.

 Master calligrapher tips

The initial ‎ح shape is raised in front of letter shapes that need to finish on the line, including و (see حو on page 31), ر and ي:

Practise writing these letter combinations containing initial and isolated ḥā', jīm and khā'.

أُغ   أُغ   أُغ   أُغ   أُغ   أُغ

جي   جي   جي   جي   جي   جي

اجزاخانة قصر النيل ajzākhāna qaṣr in-nīl (Qasr el-nil Pharmacy)

The letter **ﻩ** hā' is unusual as it changes its shape more radically than most letters when joined.

First practise tracing and then copying the isolated letter shape, making sure you move your pen *clockwise*.

start here

The isolated letter looks similar in the printed and handwritten forms:

Printed form   *Handwritten form*

_ _ **ﻩ** _ _ _ _   _ _ **ه** _ _   the letter hā'. Pronounced h as in 'hotel'.

Joining up

Pay special attention to the different shapes of **ﻩ** hā' when joined. Although the final form is recognisable, the initial and medial forms look very different.

final
*joined to the
letter before only*

medial
joined both sides

initial
*joined to the
letter after only*

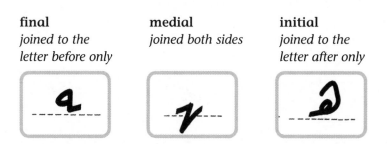

The medial form of **ھ** hā' is also significantly different in ruq'a handwriting from the printed naskh script, where it looks more like a ribbon tied in a bow:

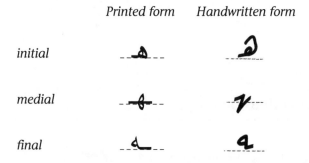

	Printed form	Handwritten form
initial		
medial		
final		

Pay special attention to the inital hā'. You need to start the letter at the top left, form a large backwards C-shape, then loop back inside the C-shape before continuing to the left.

Practise tracing and then copying the initial, medial and final forms of **ھ** hā':

☛ Master calligrapher tips

The final hā' can be also be written like this:

So ب followed by ه can be written in in either of these two ways:

Look at these words with ه hā' in the printed and handwritten forms:

Printed form   Handwritten form

            nahr *river*

            hunā *here*

وجه   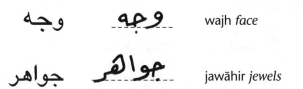   wajh *face*

جواهر   جواهر   jawāhir *jewels*

Notice how the initial ن curves round the other way into the shape of the following hā' in the handwritten نهر (river).

Practise writing those words.

ة tā' marbūta

There is a special feminine ending which looks like ه hā' with two dots on top: ة. This only ever appears at the end of words and is known as tā' marbūta ('tied t'). It is pronounced a or at.

The tā' marbūta is handwritten in exactly the same way as a final or isolated ه hā', with the addition of a dash representing the two dots:

Printed form   *Handwritten form*

هدية   ‏ــهـدـية   hadīya *present/gift*

جريدة   ‏جريدة   jarīda *newspaper*

زبدة   ‏زبدة   zubda *butter*

ــهـدـية

جريدة

زبدة

What's on the shopping list?

jarīda *newspaper*
hadiya li-hudā *present for Hoda*
bunn *coffee beans*
zayt zaytūn *olive oil*
zubda *butter*
tīn *figs*

مـ

Printed form   Handwritten form

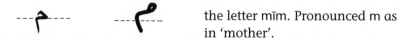

---مـ---   ---مـ---   the letter mīm. Pronounced m as in 'mother'.

The letter مـ mīm doesn't share its shape with any other letter. Notice how you start the letter shape in the middle, forming a tight circle in a clockwise direction, before continuing to the left and then downwards into the tail.

The handwritten ruq'a mīm sits a little higher than the printed naskh form, although the tail does end *below* the line.

Practise tracing and then copying the letter shape.

start here

Look at how م mīm is joined, particularly in handwriting.

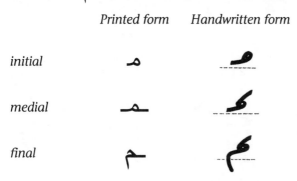

ﻢ mīm can be a tricky letter to spot, becoming 'tucked' under, or sometimes over, the surrounding letters. It takes time to recognise and practise the various combinations. In this unit, we will concentrate on the easier combinations with the initial and isolated ﻢ mīm. Unit 19 in Part 2 will show how ﻢ mīm is written in combination with specific letters.

Practise writing these combinations starting with ﻢ mīm. Remember to start the initial mīm in the same position as the isolated letter, forming a tight clockwise circle.

ما   ما   م + ا =

مد   مد   م + د =

مت   مت   م + ت =

مه   مه   م + ه =

Now practise these words ending with an isolated م mīm:

نوم نوم   nawm

خام خام   khām

ندم ندم   nadam

Masthead from the children's magazine ماجد mājid (Majid – a boy's name)

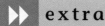

▶▶ **extra**

Hamza (ء)

The Arabic hamza (ء) is sometimes described as a 'half-letter'.
It represents the short intake of breath that an English
speaker would naturally make before a word starting with a
vowel (e.g. 'instant', 'egg'). In Arabic script, the hamza is
usually written together with an alif when a word starts with
a vowel: above the alif if the vowel is a/aa or u/ū and below if
the vowel is i/ī:

Printed form   Handwritten form

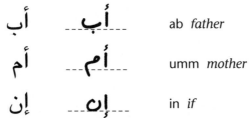

أب   ‫__أب__‬   ab *father*

أم   ‫__أم__‬   umm *mother*

إن   ‫__إن__‬   in *if*

Try writing the hamza, first by itself and then above and
under an alif. Complete the alif first before adding the hamza:

The hamza (ء) can also appear in the middle of a word representing a short pause, or at the end of a word when it has the effect of cutting off the previous sound. In these cases, the hamza can also be found written on a waw (ؤ), on a ya' without dots (ـئـ/ئ), or by itself on the line (ء):

Printed form   Handwritten form

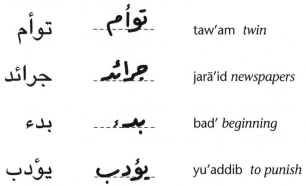

Printed	Handwritten	
توأم	ـتوأم	taw'am *twin*
جرائد	جرائد	jarā'id *newspapers*
بدء	بـدء	bad' *beginning*
يؤدب	يؤدب	yu'addib *to punish*

Practise these words containing the hamza. Write the whole word first and then add the hamza along with any dots.

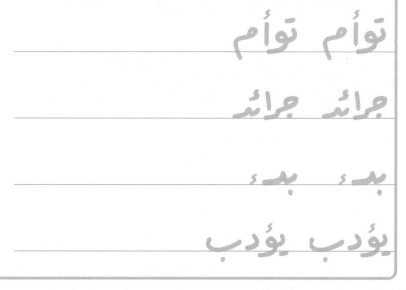

This letter shape involves three basic movements:
        a short upwards stroke
        a longer stroke to the left
        a final curved tail.
The tail is a similar movement to the final ﻦ (see Unit 2).

Practise tracing and then copying the letter shape.

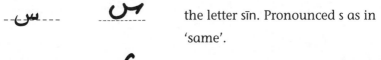

start
here

This shape is used for two Arabic letters. In their printed naskh forms, these letters start with a backwards w-shape, but this is usually 'smoothed out' in the handwritten form. Notice also how the handwritten tail sits *on* the line but the printed tail falls *below* the line.

Printed form   Handwritten form

Printed	Handwritten	
ﺲ	ﺲ	the letter sīn. Pronounced s as in 'same'.
ﺶ	ﺶ	the letter shīn. Pronounced sh as in 'shame'.

Remember to write the ^ shape representing the three dots over the shīn after completing the main letter or word shape.

Joining up

Like many Arabic letters, sīn and shīn lose their tails when joined to the next letter. Combined with the smoothing of the w-shape, this effectively turns the medial sīn and shīn into a straight line.

final	**medial**	**initial**
joined to the letter before only	*joined both sides*	*joined to the letter after only*

Notice the position of the final form, with the tail finishing on the line. The means that the previous letter(s) should be raised, so the whole combination ends back on the line:

> ✎ **Master calligrapher tips**
>
> The sīn and shīn sometimes retain the w-shape in handwriting
> especially when placed in front of ي, ـه, ج, and م:
>
>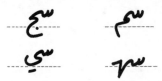

Practise combinations with sīn and shīn.

س + ه =   رسه   سه

ش + ا =   شا   شا

ب + س =   بس   بس

خ + ش =   فش   فش

ب + س + ه =   بسه   بسه

س + ي =   سي   سي

أحذية سيسيل aḥdhīyat sīsīl (Cecil shoes).

Notice the two occurrences of the letter س sīn: probably written in different styles because two straight lines would look odd.

ص ض

Practise forming the letter shape, first by tracing the shape and then by yourself. The tail is a similar shape to sīn in Unit 10. Pay special attention to where you start the initial loop:

start here

This shape is used for two Arabic letters. Compare the printed form with the handwritten. The handwritten tail sits *on* the line, while the printed tail falls *under* the line:

Printed form   Handwritten form

ـصـ   ص   the letter ṣād. The basic shape without any additional dots. Pronounced as an emphatic ṣ, similar to the 's' in the English 'sob' (rather than 'sad').

ـضـ   ض   the letter ḍād. With an additional dot above. Pronounced as an emphatic ḍ, similar to the 'd' in the English 'doll' (rather than 'dill').

Practise writing the two letters. Remember to start the loop on
the left, in the centre of the letter:

Joining up

Look closely at how the final ṣād and ḍād are joined to the letter
before and after. You should not need to take your pen off the
paper. Try tracing the path of the pen below with your finger:

final	**medial**	**initial**
joined to the letter before only	*joined both sides*	*joined to the letter after only*

    Master calligrapher tips

You can also write the isolated and final ضـ ḍād with a tail
the same shape as the alternate نـ nūn and شـ shīn (see
Units 2 and 10). If you write the ḍād with this alternative tail,
you should *not* also put a dot above the letter:

Whenever ṣād and ḍād are joined to the following letter, you
should be careful to include the small 'dink' (or سنة sinna –
'tooth' – as the Arabs call it) after the loop as this is an
essential part of the shape.

Printed form   *Handwritten form*

بيض‎   بيض‎   bayḍ   *eggs*

حضارة‎   حضارة‎   ḥaḍāra   *civilisation*

صابر‎   صابر‎   ṣābir   *patient/enduring*

مصر للبترول miṣr lil-betrūl *(Egypt Petroleum)*

Practise joining ṣād and ḍād. Remember to finish the whole shape of the word first, and then come back to add any dots.

بيض بيض بيض بيض بيض

حضارة حضارة حضارة حضارة حضارة

صابر صابر صابر صابر صابر

لا ل

This letter shape represents the Arabic letter lām:

Printed form   Handwritten form

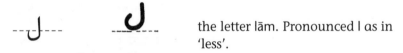

the letter lām. Pronounced l as in 'less'.

The printed naskh form of lām falls below the line, but the handwritten ruq'a form sits on the line.

Practise tracing and then copying the shape.

start
here

Joining up

The lām looks somewhat like a mirror image of the English letter 'l' and is formed in a similar way, but in the reverse direction. As with a joined-up English 'l', you must take your pen to the top of the medial and final lām first, before returning down the same path and continuing to the left.

final	**medial**	**initial**
joined to the letter before only	*joined both sides*	*joined to the letter after only*

 Master calligrapher tips

When you join to a final lām, the initial letter(s) are raised, joining to the *middle* of the lām, with the final tail of the lām ending back on the line:

$$ه + ل = هل \qquad ب + ل = بل$$

$$ج + ل = جل \qquad س + ل = سل$$

lām, along with alif, is one of the most common letters of the Arabic alphabet, as together they form the word الـ.. al- (the). الـ.. al- is written joined to the word it refers to:

Printed form	Handwritten form	
الباب	الباب	al-bāb *the door*
البومة	البومة	al-būma *the owl*
الزبدة	الزبدة	az-zubda* *the butter*

* al- is pronounced as az- in this combination.

Practise tracing and then copying the combinations with lām.

له   له   له   له   له   له   له

بل   بل   جل   بل   بل   جل   جل

الباب   الباب   الباب   الباب   الباب

البومة   البومة   البومة   البومة

الزبدة   الزبدة   الزبدة   الزبدة

ﻻ lām-alif

When the letter alif follows lām a special combined shape is produced called lām-alif:

Printed form   Handwritten form

📌 **Master calligrapher tips**

The movement used to handwrite ﻻ is similar to the movement required to write اﻟ ا:

Practise tracing ﻻ and then copying the shape.

Look at how the combinations of letters below join together:

Printed form   Handwritten form

ل + ل + ا = ‏للا‏   للا

ص + ل + ا = ‏صلا‏   صلا

س + ل + ا + م = ‏سلام‏   سلام

م + ل + ا + ب + س = ‏ملابس‏   ملابس

Trace then copy the combinations with lām alif.

Masthead from the Lebanese newpaper الأنوار al-anwār (The Lights)

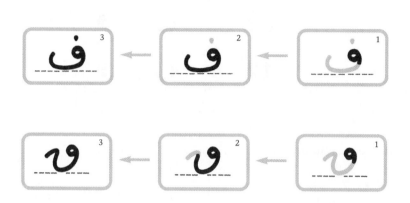

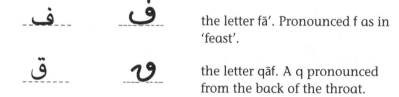

Printed form   Handwritten form

the letter fā'. Pronounced f as in 'feast'.

the letter qāf. A q pronounced from the back of the throat.

These two letters are related but look somewhat different in their isolated forms.

The tail of the qāf is rounder and, in ruq'a handwriting, the two dots are usually written as a flourish on the end of the tail, similar to the alternate nūn, shīn and ḍād.

Master calligrapher tips

ف is the shape of ب joined to the head of و.
ق is the shape of the ن joined to the head of the و.

Practise tracing and then copying the letter shapes.

start
here

start
here

Joining up

When fā' and qāf are joined to the letter before, i.e. in the initial or medial forms, their shape is identical. The only difference is that fā' has one dot and qāf a dash, representing two dots. Pay attention to how the loop is formed in the medial letter.

In the final form, the letters are a similar shape to their isolated forms.

final	**medial**	**initial**
joined to the letter before only	*joined both sides*	*joined to the letter after only*

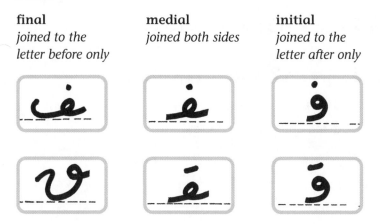

Notice the difference in the height above the line of the previous letter as it joins the final fā' and qāf.

$$\underline{\;بِف\;} = ف + ب$$

$$\underline{\;بِق\;} = ق + ب$$

Compare these handwritten words with their printed forms:

Printed form   Handwritten form

فريق   فريق   farīq   *team*

قفل   قَفَل   qafl   *lock*

صقر	صقـر	saqr *hawk*
ثقافة	ثَقَافة	thaqāfa *culture*
فرق	فرق	farq *difference*
دقيق	دقَيق	daqīq *flour*
دقائق	دقَائُق	daqā'iq *minutes*

Practise tracing and copying those words.

ثَقَافةَ ثَقَافةَ ثَقَافةَ ثَقَافةَ ثَقَافةَ

فروه فروه فروه فروه فروه

دقيه دقيه دقيه دقيه دقيه

دقائُه دقائُه دقائُه دقائُه دقائُه

extra

Numbers

The figures 1, 2, 3, 4, etc. used in European languages are based on Arabic numbers and are often termed 'Arabic' numerals (as opposed to 'Latin' numerals i, ii, iii, iv, etc.). However, the figures commonly used in the Arab world vary somewhat from their European counterparts:

	Printed	*Handwritten*	
0	•	•	ṣifr صفر
1	١	١	wāḥid واحد
2	٢	٢	ithnān اثنان
3	٣	٣	thalātha ثلاثة
4	٤	٤	arbaع a أربعة
5	٥	٥	khamsa خمسة
6	٦	٦	sitta ستّة
7	٧	٧	sabع a سبعة
8	٨	٨	thamānya ثمانية
9	٩	٩	tisع a تسعة
10	١٠	١٠	ع ashara عشرة

If you look how ١٠ (10) is written, you can see that Arabic numbers read from left to right as in English – the opposite direction to the rest of the script.

Handwritten Arabic numbers look similar to the printed ones. The main exception is the number 2. Note also that sometimes a hastily handwritten Arabic three ٣ looks more like a printed two ٢. Watch out for this as it can be confusing.

Practise writing the Arabic numbers, starting at the black dot:

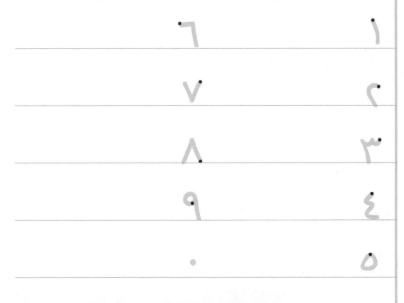

What's the registration number of this Cairo taxi?

ك

The letter ك kāf does not share its shape with any other letter.

Compare the usual printed and handwritten forms. Notice how the handwritten version usually joins the hamza shape in the middle of the letter to create a clockwise swirl:

Printed form   Handwritten form

ك   ك   the letter kāf. Pronounced k as in 'kettle'.

Master calligrapher tips

The movement required to produce the handwritten kāf is similar to a combination of the shapes used to produce ا followed by ب followed by د:

$$ ك = د ب ا $$

First practise tracing and then copying the isolated letter shape, making sure you follow the direction shown in the numbered sequence at the top of the page.

start
here

Joining up

Pay special attention to the different shapes of the letter ك kāf when joined. The final form is recognisable, but the initial and medial forms look different.

final	**medial**	**initial**
joined to the letter before only	*joined both sides*	*joined to the letter after only*

Practise the medial and final forms of kāf, following the arrows and completing the downwards angled stroke *last*.

  Master calligrapher tips

The initial and medial kāf is written in a semi-circular shape before an ascending letter, such as ا, another ك or ل:

When writing words containing initial or medial kāfs you should write the lower part of the letter, but leave the upper slanted stroke as an addition to be completed when you have finished the whole shape of the word, along with any dots on other letters:

Stage 1: لراطا

Stage 2: كراكات (karrākāt)

This is similar to how joined-up 't's and 'i's are formed in English, with the main vertical strokes completed as part of the word, and the letters crossed and dotted at the end:

Stage 1: *brule*

Stage 2: *trite*

Look at these words with ك kāf in their printed and handwritten forms:

Printed form   Handwritten form

Printed	Handwritten	
كرة	كرة	kura *ball*
كل	كل	kull *all, every*
شكل	شكل	shakl *shape*
ديك	ديك	dīk *cockerel*
مفك	مفك	mifakk *screwdriver*

Now practise writing those words.

كرة كرة

كل كل

شكل شكل

ديك ديك

مفك مفك

الكاف تَكتب بهذا الشكل الدائري

إذا كانه بعدها حرف صاعد

الكاف تكتب بهذا الشكل الدائري إذا كان بعدها حرف صاعد

al-kāf tuktab bi-hādhā sh-shakl id-dā'irī idhā kāna baᶜdahā harf ṣāᶜid
('The kāf is written in this circular shape if after it there is an
ascending letter.')

Original Arabic text of the Master calligrapher tip on page 65
written by Professor Mohammed Hamaam. Notice how the
slanting stokes of the kāfs have become slightly separated from
the lower part of the letters, showing that they have been
added at a later stage.

Practise forming the letter shape, first by tracing the shape and then by yourself. You should form the loop at the bottom first in a clockwise direction, and then add the vertical stroke downwards:

This shape is used for two Arabic letters. The printed and handwritten versions look similar.

Printed	Handwritten	
ط	ط	the letter ṭā'. The basic shape without any additional dots. Pronounced as an emphatic ṭ, similar to the 't' in the English 'ṭold' (rather than 'ṭen').
ظ	ظ	the letter ẓā'. With an additional dot above. Pronounced as an emphatic ẓ, a cross between 'z' and 'th' pronounced with the tongue in a similar position to other emphatic letters such as ṭā'.

Practise writing the two letters. Remember to add the downward stroke and the dot last.

Joining up

ط and ظ look similar wherever they appear in a word. Notice that when you join them to the letter *before*, i.e. in the medial and final forms, you need to loop back over the line before continuing.

final	**medial**	**initial**
joined to the letter before only	*joined both sides*	*joined to the letter after only*

  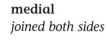

Practise writing the words below. As with the letter kāf (see Unit 14), it's best to complete an entire word and then add the downward stroke of the ط or ظ, along with any dots.

 ṭaha

 baṭṭ

 ẓill

حظك   ḥaẓẓak

الطلاق   aṭ-ṭalāq

بطاطس   baṭāṭis

Can you read the signs on the vegetables?

(potatoes)	(carrots)	(tomatoes)	(celery)	(onions)
baṭāṭis	jazar	ṭamāṭim	karafs	basal
بطاطس	جزر	طماطم	كرفس	بصل

 غ ع

The initial section of this letter shape is similar to the shape of the hamza (see *extra* pages 42–3). The tail finishes below the line.

Practise forming the letter shape:

start
here

🖋 Master calligrapher tips

In ruq'a handwriting there are only three letter shapes which have tails falling below the line:

This shape is used for two Arabic letters. The printed and handwritten versions look similar.

Printed   *Handwritten*

--ع--   --ع--   the letter ‛ayn. A guttural letter difficult to pronounce. Sounds like 'ah' coming from the stomach.

--غ--   --غ--   the letter ghayn. With an additional dot above. Pronounced as an 'r' from the back of the throat as in the French 'rouge'.

Practise writing the two letters.

Joining up

final   **medial**   **initial**
joined to the   *joined both sides*   *joined to the*
letter before only   *letter after only*

The initial form is similar to the isolated form, but without the final tail. The medial and final forms have a modified shape in both printed and handwritten Arabic: a small triangular loop. Joining from the right you need to curve up slightly, then loop back to the right before continuing curving down again to the left.

Notice that, in common with other letters with a final tail, the handwritten ع is raised higher to enable the tail to finish in the correct position. This will have the effect of also raising the letter(s) before:

$$\text{--}\underline{\hspace{1em}}\text{ع} = \text{ع} + \text{ب}$$

Practise writing the words containing ع and غ in different positions:

نوع nawع

يبلغك yuballighak

علامة عalāma

مشاغل mashāghil

دكتور خالد كمال
duktūr khālid kamāl
(Doctor Khalid Kamal)
دكتور سعيد حسن
duktūr saعīd ḥasan
(Doctor Saeed Hasan)

You have now covered all the basic letter shapes needed to write Arabic. You will find the complete table of all the letters in the various positions on pages 112–16. Part 2 deals with how to form particular combinations of letters and Part 3 gives you a chance to put all you have learnt into practice.

Letter combinations

17 General principles

Working your way through Part 1 of this book, you have already encountered some of the general principles involved in handwriting Arabic. Here is a summary of the main points you have met:

- Double and treble dots above and below letters become dashes and 'caps': ‸ ⁃ .

- The 'w' shape at the beginning of sīn س and shīn ش generally becomes a smooth line: ﺳ .

- Some final letters have alternative final forms, e.g. ﺻ / ﺿ , ﺳ / ﺵ , ﻢ / ﻦ , and ﻦ / ﻦ .

- Each group of letters needs to end with the final character in the correct position on the line – the height of preceding letters should be adjusted to achieve this.

- In addition, some special shapes have developed to join particular combinations of letters.

Implementing all of these principles requires practice and time. You will start by only recognising some of the more complicated combinations. However, the more you can apply the principles, the more your handwriting will resemble that of a native Arabic speaker, and so the more credibility you will acquire. You need to imagine how you would regard a foreigner who writes you an English note in printed infant letters as opposed to a fully formed adult hand.

Final letters

In this unit we will look as a whole at final letters and how they affect the letters that come before. The 'final letter' could be the last letter in a word or it could be a non-joining letter, making it the last letter in a combination.

Some final letters are written along the line and there is no special adjustment needed to the letter(s) that come before:

$$بِفْ = ف + ب$$

$$مفك = ك + ف + م$$

$$جيا = ا + ي + ج$$

But others are joined higher to allow the final tail to fall in the correct position:

$$بوق = ق + ب$$

$$فل = ل + ف$$

$$جر = ر + ج$$

Compare the position of the initial bā' ـب in بف and بق above. When joining to fā' ف you can start the bā' on the line, but when joining to qāf ق you should raise the bā' in anticipation, so that the deeper tail of the qāf falls back on the line. The ability to anticipate is one of the features of good Arabic handwriting.

Here are the final letters like qāf that are joined to above the line:

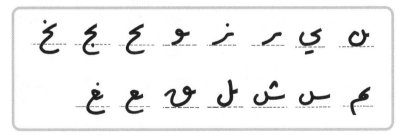

Units 18–20 will cover joining to ج/ح/خ, م and ي. In this unit we will practise the other final letters.

Practise tracing and copying these combinations, taking care to
start the initial letter above the line:

Now trace and write these complete words taking note of the
relative positions of the letters.

جبل جبل   jabal

قفل قفل   qafl

فريق فريق   farīq

تـلل تـلل   tasallul

جواهر جواهر   jawāhir

unit 18 — Joining to ح

In Unit 7 you saw how the initial letter shape ﺟ joins to following letters. This shape is shared by the letters ج jīm, ح hā' and خ khā'.

In this unit we will look in more detail at the medial and final shapes for these letters.

final	**medial**	**initial**
joined to the letter before only	*joined both sides*	*joined to the letter after only*

You can see that the medial and final letter shapes are joined to the letter before with a diagonal right-to-left stroke joining at the top left-hand side of the main letter. This requires anticipation when joining.

Practise tracing and copying the medial and final shapes, taking care to start where indicated by the arrow:

There is also a special combined shape used when ـب (or any of
the letters which share its initial and medial shape – see Unit 3)
is joined to ج jīm, ح hā' or خ khā':

$$ـجـ = جـ + ـب$$

$$ـحـ = حـ + ـب$$

Practise these combinations:

ـجـ   ـحـ   ـجـ   ـحـ   ـجـ   ـحـ   ـجـ

الاتحاد al-ittiḥād (The Union)
Masthead from the Emirates-based newspaper

Compare these words in their printed and handwritten forms.

Printed form   Handwritten form

بحار   بحار   biḥār *seas*

مجلات   مجلات   majallāt *magazines*

ريح   ريح   rīḥ *wind*

بخيل   بخيل   bakhīl *miser*

مناهج   مناهج   manāhij *methods/procedures*

Now try writing the words for yourself:

_____   بحار

_____   مجلات

_____   ريح

_____   بخيل

_____   مناهج

مطعم الحاتي matˤam al-ḥātī (Al-Hati Restaurant)
Notice how the ل is joined to the top left of the ح,
and how several letters have ornamental upwards
strokes for decorative effect.

Joining to

The letter mīm ـم is one of the trickiest letters to master. You have already seen in Unit 9 that when it loses its tail it is reduced to a small circle or blob:

mīm in isolation:

initial mīm:

In addition, when mīm is in the medial or final position, with a letter following it, it tends to become tucked *under* the letter in handwriting, sometimes making it difficult to spot:

final	**medial**	**initial**
joined to the letter before only	*joined both sides*	*joined to the letter after only*

Practise forming the medial and final shapes, completing the black part of the shape first. You can move your pen around on the spot until you can see a blob, especially if using a thinner nib.

Look at how these letters join to mīm:

$$\underline{-\acute{\varphi}} = \varphi + \zeta$$

$$\underline{-\acute{\varphi}.} = \varphi + \text{ب}$$

$$\underline{! \overset{\scriptstyle\smallfrown}{}} = \varphi + \text{س} + \text{ا}$$

$$\underline{\text{ملك}} = \text{ك} + \varphi + \text{س}$$

Certain combinations of mīm and other letters can result in a 'pile up' of three or four letters above the line.

$$\underline{-\acute{\underset{\smile}{\smile}}} = \text{ر} + \varphi + \text{ت}$$

$$\underline{-\underset{\smile}{\overset{\cdot}{\smile}}} = \varphi + \text{ي} + \text{خ} + \varphi$$

If you can write these kinds of combinations correctly and fluently, you can truly claim to have mastered Arabic handwriting!

Practise forming those combinations:

سمك

تمر

مخيم

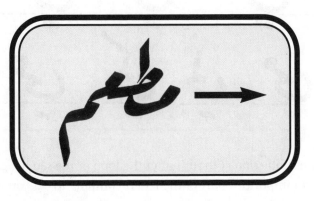

مطعم maṭɛam (restaurant)

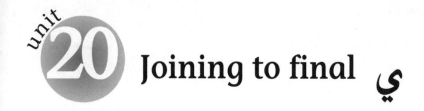
In Unit 3 you saw how the initial بـ shape combines with a
final yā' to produce this shape: بي .

Other letters combine with the final yā' in a similar way. Look at
how the final yā' combines with these ten initial letter shapes:

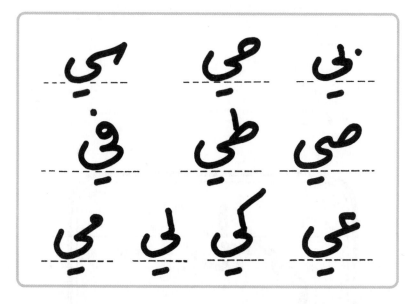

Note the subtle sinna ('tooth') after the loop of the ṣād in صي.
This is an important part of the letter (compare to طي on its
left). In addition, don't forget to add any dots and the
downwards stroke of the ط and ك *after* you have completed the
whole of the main shape.

Try tracing and then copying those shapes. Start at the black dot.

بي حي ٺي بي حي ٺي

في طي صي في طي صي

مي لي كي عي مي لي كي عي

The banner across the magazine reads:

إقرأوا في هذا العدد iqra'ū fī hādhā l-ع adad (Read in this issue).

Notice how the word في fī (in) is written.

21 Summary of combinations with ـبـ

As a summary of how Arabic letters combine, look at the following which shows the initial ـبـ joined to all the letters of the alphabet in turn in their final forms (see pages 112–16 for the Arabic letters in alphabetical order).

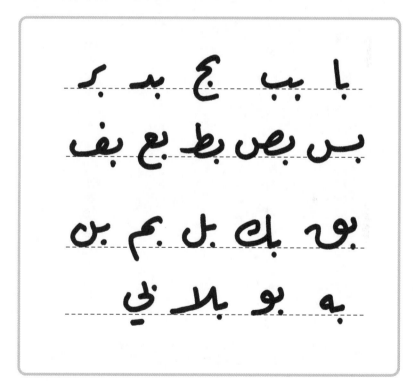

Compare particularly the position of the ـبـ in relation to the letter that follows: the point and height above the line at which it joins.

Now practise copying these combinations:

با بب جـ بـد بر

بـس بص بط بع بف

بو بك بل بم بن

به بو بلا بي

By working your way through this guide, you should now have mastered the fundamentals of reading and writing ruq'a Arabic script. In Part 3, you will find activities which will further improve your script and provide you with practice in deciphering handwritten material.

Write on!

Activities for further practice

The **Write on!** section consists of additional activities designed
to provide further practice in handwriting and recognition. You
will find the answers to these activities on page 106.

Activity 1

Handwrite these combination of letters, as in the example.

جا   = ١ + ج

_____   = ه + م

_____   = ب + ض =

_____   = ش + ك =

_____   = ف + ل =

_____   = ك + ل =

_____   = ل + ١ =

_____   = ط + س =

_____   = ت + ع =

_____   = ب + ي =

Activity 2

Now write these printed naskh words in ruq'a script, as in the example.

سكان (sukkān) = سكان ــــــــــــــــــــــــ

جهـات (jihāt) = ــــــــــــــــــــــــ

حفـار (ḥaffār) = ــــــــــــــــــــــــ

شكل (shakl) = ــــــــــــــــــــــــ

بحل (biḥall) = ــــــــــــــــــــــــ

أحبك (uḥibbak) = ــــــــــــــــــــــــ

تسلل (tasallul) = ــــــــــــــــــــــــ

سبـائك (sabā'ik) = ــــــــــــــــــــــــ

مشـاغل (mashāghil) = ــــــــــــــــــــــــ

الجمـال (al-jamāl) = ــــــــــــــــــــــــ

Activity 3

Match the handwritten words with their printed equivalents, as in the example.

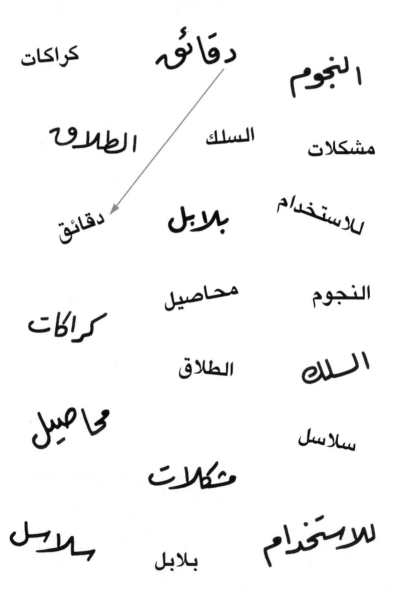

كراكات   دقَائُه   النجوم

الطلاق   السلك   مشكلات

دقائق   بلابل   للاستخدام

كراكات   محاصيل   النجوم

مشكلات   الطلاق   السلك

محاصيل   سلاسل

سلاسل   بلابل   للاستخدام

Activity 4

Now write the words from Activity 3 on the lines.

السلك (as-silk)

الطلاق (aṭ-ṭalāq)

النجوم (an-nujūm)

سلاسل (salāsil)

بلابل (balābil)

دقائق (daqā'iq)

محاصيل (maḥāṣīl)

كراكات (karrākāt)

للاستخدام (lil-istikhdām)

مشكلات (mushkilāt)

Activity 5

Can you work out the names and nationalities of these three travellers from their immigration forms?

الاسم name : .... رياصم صبري ....

الجنسية nationality : .... كويتي ....

الاسم name : .... نادية بدوي ....

الجنسية nationality : .... تونـــية ....

الاسم name : .... محمد خالد ....

الجنسية nationality : .... عراقي ....

Activity 6

How many kilometres is it to these towns?

Minya   al-minyā المنيا

Luxor   al-uqṣur الأقصر

Beni Suef   banī swayf بني سويف

Cairo   al-qāhira القاهرة

Asyut   asyūṭ أسيوط

Al Fayoum   al-fayūm الفيوم

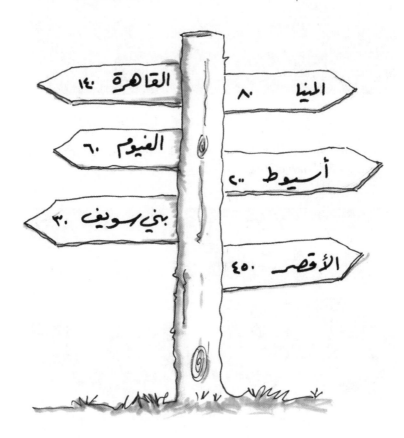

Activity 7

a) Can you work out the name of this pasta (مكرونة) company?

b) And how about this doctor? (*hint*: the Arabic name Amr is spelt with a silent wāw on the end: عمرو)

Activity 8

How much would the following cost you in the Marina cafeteria?

Pizza and ice cream?

Spaghetti and kebab?

Tuna mayonnaise and cappuccino?

Activity 9

Circle the following places in the box below, as in the example:

Madrid ✔
Crete
London
Peru
Aswan
Athens
Majorca
Mauritania
Oman
Liverpool (*hint*: the foreign sound 'v' is often written in Arabic
as a ف fā' with three dots: ڤ)

كريت سردينيا مايوركا سيدني

ناميبيا الجولا بيرو موريتانيا

مدريد لندن عمان أثينا

أجاحي سامبراس بيكر شوماخر

ليفربول أسوان ليدز جلاسجو

Activity 10

Look at the travel agent's window and answer these questions:

1. Is the agent offering a package to New York?
2. What ancient site is included in the travel package to Aswan?
3. The package to the Far East includes five nights in Thailand and four nights in which place?
4. How many nights can you stay in Berlin?
5. Which Japanese and European cities can you visit on a five-star package?

Activity 11

juice	عصير aṣīr ع
natural	طبيعي ṭabīʿ ī
oranges	برتقال butuqāl
carrots	جزر jazar
strawberries	فراولة farāwla
mangos	مانجو māngo
guavas	جوافة gawāfa
tamarind	تمر هندي tamr hindī
sugar cane	قصب qaṣab

Look at the photo of the juice stall opposite and the word list above. Then see if you can work out how much these juices cost.

1. one orange juice
2. two tamarind juices
3. one strawberry juice
4. one juice cocktail
5. two guava juices
6. two carrot juices
7. three mango juices
8. four sugar cane juices

Answers to the Activities

Activity 1   *Activity 2*

ج + ا = ‏جا‎   سكان = ‏سكان‎

م + ه = ‏مه‎   جهات = ‏جهات‎

ب + ض = ‏بض‎   حفار = ‏حفار‎

ش + ك = ‏شك‎   شكل = ‏شكل‎

ف + ل = ‏فل‎   بحل = ‏بحل‎

ك + ل = ‏كل‎   أحبك = ‏أحبك‎

ل + ا = ‏لا‎   تسلل = ‏تسلل‎

ط + س = ‏طس‎   سبائك = ‏سبائك‎

ت + ع = ‏تع‎   مشاغل = ‏مشاغل‎

ب + ي = ‏بي‎   الجمال = ‏الجمال‎

Activity 3

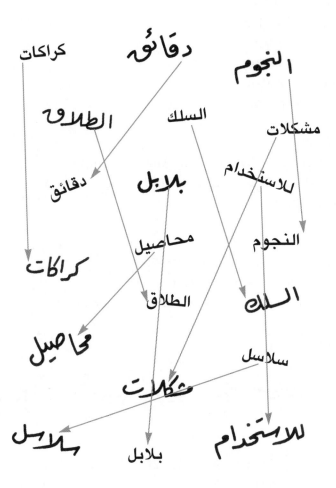

Activity 5

1. Riyad Sabri (رياض صبري); Bahraini (بحريني)
2. Nadya Badawi (نادية بدوي); Tunisian (تونسية)
3. Muhammad Khalid (محمد خالد); Iraqi (عراقي)

Activity 6

Minya	80km
Luxor	450km
Beni Suef	30km
Cairo	140km
Asyut	200km
Al Fayoum	60km

Activity 7

a) مينا القاهرة mīna al-qāhira (Mina of Cairo)

b) دكتور عمرو عبد الفتاح duktūr ٬amr ٬abd al-fattāḥ (Dr Amr Abd al-Fattah)

Activity 8

Pizza and ice cream = 750 (550 + 200)
Spaghetti and kebab = 710 (290 + 420)
Tuna mayonnaise and cappuccino = 480 (365 + 115)

Activity 9

Activity 10

1. Yes (top of window: middle poster: نيو يورك)
2. Abu Simbel (أبو سمبل)
3. Bali (بالي)
4. 3 nights (٣ ليال)
5. Tokyo (طوكيو), Osaka (اوزاكا) and Vienna (ڤيينا)

Activity 11

1. one orange juice = 50

2. two tamarind juices = 50 (25 x 2)

3. one strawberry juice = 100

4. one juice cocktail = 100

5. two guava juices = 200 (100 x 2)

6. two carrot juices = 100 (50 x 2)

7. three mango juices = 300 (100 x 3)

8. four sugar cane juices = 100 (25 x 4)

Arabic alphabet
Summary table

This reference table presents a summary of the 28 handwritten and printed Arabic letters in alphabetical order. The letters are shown in their various forms.

You will find details of the discretionary vowel and doubling signs in the *extra* section on pages 14–15.

The *extra* section on pages 42–43 covers how to write the Arabic hamza (ء).

final	*medial*	*initial*	*isolated*	*letter*
ل	ل	ا	ا	ألف alif *printed* (naskh)
ل	ل	ا	ا	*handwritten* (ruq'a)
ب	ب	ب	ب	باء bā' *printed* (naskh)
ب	ب	ب	ب	*handwritten* (ruq'a)
ت	ت	ت	ت	تاء tā' *printed* (naskh)
ت	ت	ت	ت	*handwritten* (ruq'a)
ث	ث	ث	ث	ثاء thā' *printed* (naskh)
ث	ث	ث	ث	*handwritten* (ruq'a)

final	medial	initial	isolated	letter

جيم jīm
printed (naskh)

handwritten (ruq'a)

حاء ḥā'
printed (naskh)

handwritten (ruq'a)

خاء khā'
printed (naskh)

handwritten (ruq'a)

دال dāl
printed (naskh)

handwritten (ruq'a)

ذال dhāl
printed (naskh)

handwritten (ruq'a)

راء rā'
printed (naskh)

handwritten (ruq'a)

final	*medial*	*initial*	*isolated*	*letter*
ـز	ـزـ	ز	ز	زاى zāy
				printed (naskh)
ـز	ـزـ	ز	ز	handwritten (ruq'a)
ـس	ـسـ	سـ	س	سين sīn
				printed (naskh)
ـس	ـ	ـ	س	handwritten (ruq'a)
ـش	ـشـ	شـ	ش	شين shīn
				printed (naskh)
ـش	ـشـ	ـش	ش	handwritten (ruq'a)
ـص	ـصـ	صـ	ص	صاد ṣād
				printed (naskh)
ـص	ـصـ	صـ	ص	handwritten (ruq'a)
ـض	ـضـ	ضـ	ض	ضاد ḍād
				printed (naskh)
ـض	ـضـ	ضـ	ض	handwritten (ruq'a)
ـط	ـطـ	طـ	ط	طاء ṭā'
				printed (naskh)
ـط	ـطـ	طـ	ط	handwritten (ruq'a)

final	medial	initial	isolated	letter
ظ	ظ	ظ	ظ	ظاء ẓā' *printed (naskh)*
ط	ظ	ظ	ظ	*handwritten (ruq'a)*
ع	ع	ع	ع	عين ʿayn *printed (naskh)*
ع	ع	ع	ع	*handwritten (ruq'a)*
غ	غ	غ	غ	غين ghayn *printed (naskh)*
غ	غ	غ	غ	*handwritten (ruq'a)*
ف	ف	ف	ف	فاء fā' *printed (naskh)*
ف	ف	ف	ف	*handwritten (ruq'a)*
ق	ق	ق	ق	قاف qāf *printed (naskh)*
ق	ق	ق	ق	*handwritten (ruq'a)*
ك	ك	ك	ك	كاف kāf *printed (naskh)*
ك	ك	ك	ك	*handwritten (ruq'a)*

final	medial	initial	isolated	letter
لـ	ـلـ	لـ	ل	لم lām *printed* (naskh)
لـ	ـلـ	لـ	ل	*handwritten* (ruq'a)
ـم	ـمـ	مـ	م	ميم mīm *printed* (naskh)
ـم	ـمـ	مـ	م	*handwritten* (ruq'a)
ـن	ـنـ	نـ	ن	نون nūn *printed* (naskh)
ـن	ـنـ	نـ	ن	*handwritten* (ruq'a)
ـه	ـهـ	هـ	ه	هاء hā' *printed* (naskh)
ـه	ـهـ	هـ	ه	*handwritten* (ruq'a)
ـو	ـو	و	و	واو wāw *printed* (naskh)
ـو	ـو	و	و	*handwritten* (ruq'a)
ـي	ـيـ	يـ	ي	ياء yā' *printed* (naskh)
ـي	ـيـ	يـ	ي	*handwritten* (ruq'a)